Map of Ancient Egypt

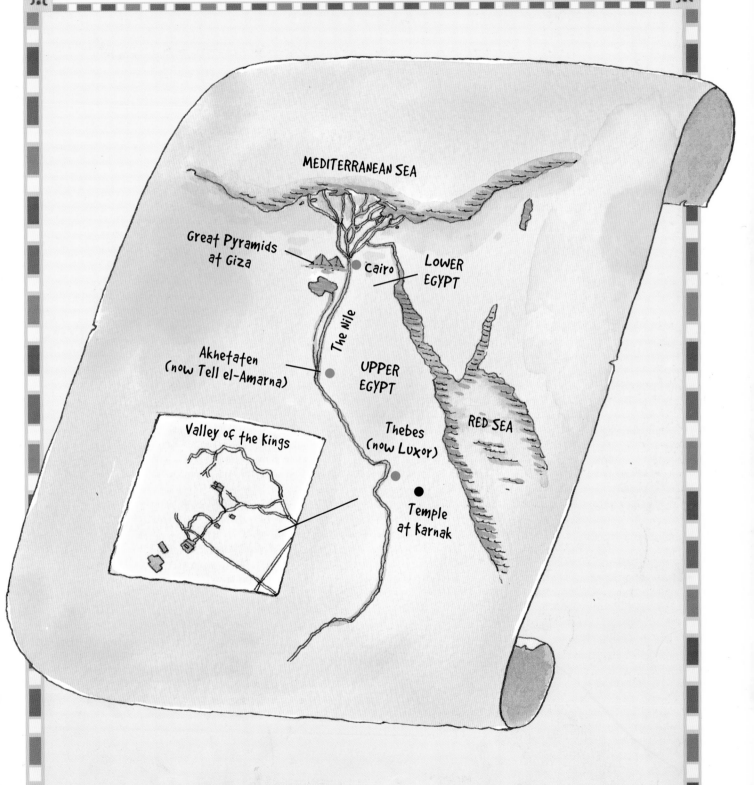

MEDITERRANEAN SEA

Great Pyramids
at Giza

Cairo

LOWER
EGYPT

The Nile

Akhetaten
(now Tell el-Amarna)

UPPER
EGYPT

RED SEA

Valley of the Kings

Thebes
(now Luxor)

Temple
at Karnak

First published in Great Britain in 2003 by Brimax
An imprint of Octopus Publishing Group Ltd
2-4 Heron Quays, London E14 4JP

© Octopus Publishing Group Ltd

A CIP catalogue record for this book is available from the British Library.

ISBN 185854 482 3 (hardback)
ISBN 185854 706 7 (paperback)

Created by *ticktock* Media Ltd.

Printed in China

932

Tutankhamun timeline

2650 BC — The first pyramid (with stepped sides) is built at Saqqara by King Zoser.

The great pyramid at Giza is — **2570 BC** — built by Pharaoh Khufu.

1352 BC — Akhenaten becomes Pharaoh.

Akhenaten orders a new capital — **1347 BC** — city to be built. He calls it Akhetaten (now called Tell el-amarna)

1345 BC — Around this time Tutankhamun is born.

Akhenaten dies and Tutankhamun — **1336 BC** — becomes Pharaoh. He marries his half-sister Ankhesenamun.

1327 BC — Tutankhamun dies aged 17 or 18. He is buried in the Valley of the Kings.

BC/AD

Archaeologists begin excavations, — **1800s AD** — in the Valley of the Kings, in Egypt.

1922 AD — Howard Carter and his team discover Tutankhamun's tomb. It has been hidden for over 3,000 years.

Howard Carter's team open — **1923 AD** — up the burial chamber and find Tutankhamun's mummy.

1932 AD — After ten years work emptying the tomb, Tutankhamun's treasures go on display in the Cairo Museum.

Howard Carter dies. — **1939 AD**

TUTANKHAMUN,
THE BOY KING

By Jackie Gaff

Illustrated by Anthony Lewis

CONTENTS

BRIMAX

Birth of a royal baby

More than 3,300 years ago, in around 1345 BC, a baby boy was born in the royal household of the **pharaoh** (or king) of ancient Egypt. The baby was given the name of Tutankhamun, and he grew up to be one of Egypt's most famous pharaohs. Although Tutankhamun's name is very well known, there have been disagreements amongst experts about who his parents were.

Some experts think that Tutankhamun was the younger brother of the ruling pharaoh, **Akhenaten**, but most now think that he was the son of Akhenaten and one of his wives, Queen **Kiya**. What is certain is that Tutankhamun was a royal prince, and that he was born into a life of wealth and power.

The pharaohs of ancient Egypt often had many wives. Akhenaten's chief wife wasn't Kiya, but the beautiful **Nefertiti**. Tutankhamun had lots of older half-sisters because, although Nefertiti had no sons, she gave birth to six daughters!

TUTANKHAMUN'S TOYS

Ancient Egyptian children played with all sorts of home-made toys – from balls and wooden dolls to model animals with moving parts and spinning tops. Some games, such as leapfrog and tug-of-war, are still played by children today.

As a boy, Tutankhamun would have lived in one of the magnificent palaces in the splendid new capital city built by Pharaoh Akhenaten. The city was named **Akhetaten** in his honour, but today the ruins are known as **Tell el-Amarna**. Most of the buildings in the city were made from mud bricks, with stone only being used to build temples. Ordinary Egyptian homes had just two or three rooms with a roof terrace on top, but the pharaoh's palaces had ten times that many, all beautifully furnished and decorated with wall paintings of flowers and animals. Ordinary Egyptians had to work very hard to survive, but Tutankhamun lived in luxury, waited on hand–and–foot by an army of slaves and servants.

A time of change

Tutankhamun was born during a very unusual period in Egypt's history. Akhenaten made some revolutionary changes to ancient Egyptian traditions. He not only built his new city Akhetaten, moving his court there from the old capital city of **Thebes**, but caused even more disruption when he introduced a new religion to his kingdom. Traditionally, the ancient Egyptians believed in hundreds of different gods, ruled over by a chief god called **Amun-Re**. But when Akhenaten was crowned pharaoh, he commanded his people to worship a single new god and abandon the old gods. The new god was a sun god, called **Aten**. Akhenaten's new religion continued until his death, when the new Pharaoh, Tutankhamun, brought back the old gods.

A NEW ART STYLE

In statues and wall carvings, Akhenaten has a long bony face and thin neck. No one knows whether Akhenaten really was so odd-looking or whether these strange images were due to the new art styles that he developed during his reign – now called **Amarna art**. *This change from traditional Egyptian art was yet another way for Akhenaten to show that he wanted to do things differently.*

8

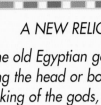

A NEW RELIGION

Many of the old Egyptian gods were portrayed as having the head or body of an animal. However, the king of the gods, Amun-Re, was usually shown as a man wearing a false beard and a crown-like headdress capped by two tall feathers. In the new religion Aten wasn't shown in human form, but as the circular disc of the sun, with long rays coming off it.

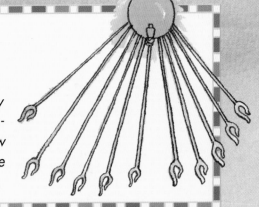

My weird ancestors by Tutankhamun *

I'd never dare say it to his face, of course, but Akhenaten isn't the only oddball pharaoh in our country's history.

Akhenaten's dad, Amenhotep III, was famous for his tall tales about big-game hunting. He claimed to have killed 102 lions in ten years!

Pharaoh Khufu may have built the Great Pyramid at Giza, but he was also a bit of a nutter. Old stories tell how he had a man's head cut off to see whether a magician could bring the dead back to life!

Statues may show Pharaoh Hatshepsut dressed as a man and wearing a beard, but this ruler was actually a woman!

* At least this is what we think Tutankhamun might have thought about his strange ancestors!

To make sure everyone switched to worshipping Aten, Akhenaten ordered the old gods' temples to be shut down, and had new temples to the sun god built in their place. The priests and the people weren't very happy about these changes to their religious traditions, but Akhenaten ignored any signs of unrest. Once Akhetaten was built, Akhenaten never stepped outside the walls of the new capital city, and paid little attention to what was happening in the rest of his kingdom.

Schooldays

Tutankhamun's schooling began when he was about five years old. As a prince, he was taught by a royal tutor, alongside the sons of the top officials at Akhenaten's court. Reading and writing were highly-prized skills in ancient Egyptian times, and only upper-class boys were taught them. All the top government jobs in ancient Egypt went to educated men who were able to read and write. They were called **scribes** and were considered one of the most important groups in society. The sons of craftsmen and farmers didn't go to school, but began learning their father's trade when they were about 12 years old instead. And although royal princesses sometimes studied alongside their brothers, most ordinary girls stayed at home and were taught housekeeping skills by their mothers.

How to make papyrus paper
by Tutankhamun *

What would we Egyptians do without papyrus? This tall reed grows wild along the banks of our river Nile. My people use it to make boats, sandals, baskets, and, of course, paper. Papermaking is a very fiddly job, and I'm glad I'll never have to do it! First of all, the reed stems are peeled and sliced into thin strips. These are bashed flat, then laid on top of each other in a crisscross pattern. A heavy weight is laid on top and the whole lot is left to dry in the sun. Like magic, the strips stick together as they dry and you end up with a sheet of papyrus paper. You can either write on single sheets, or join several together to make a long scroll – very clever!

* We think Tutankhamun might have written an essay like this at school!

Schoolmasters were very strict too, and the boys would receive a beating if they misbehaved. Tutankhamun would have been taught mathematics from a young age as well, starting with simple sums and working up to more complex subjects such as geometry. Once he'd mastered reading and writing using the Egyptian alphabet of **hieroglyphs**, Tutankhamun would have gone on to study everything from history and geography to **astronomy**.

WRITING EQUIPMENT

A scribe's basic writing equipment was a palette with two hollows for cakes of solid red, blue or black ink, and a small stone pot to hold water for wetting the ink. The scribe's reed pens sat in a groove in the palette, along with a knife for trimming sheets of **papyrus** paper.

HIEROGLYPHS

Learning to read and write ancient Egyptian was very tricky. Instead of the 26 letters of our modern-day alphabet, the Egyptians wrote with picture symbols called hieroglyphs. Schoolboys had to learn more than 700 of them off by heart!

fun and games

Life was not all study and school for the young Tutankhamun. Sport was another important part of his education, and plenty of time was allowed for running, rowing, swimming, and wrestling. Like all Egyptian cities, Akhetaten was built close to the banks of the **Nile**, and Tutankhamun would have spent many a hot afternoon splashing about in the river, learning to swim. He wouldn't have been allowed there on his own, though. The Nile was a dangerous place in ancient Egyptian times, home to man-eating crocodiles and huge hippos. Egyptian noblemen liked to risk their lives trying to spear the hippos and crocodiles from small reed river-boats.

CHARIOTS AND HUNTING

Tutankhamun began learning how to drive a chariot when he was about eight. When he was older, he rode with a **charioteer** into the desert on hunting expeditions. The driver would control the horses so Tutankhamun could shoot his spears and arrows at wild animals. These weapons were incredibly sharp, tipped with ivory, bone, flint, or metal.

Rich Egyptians also rode their chariots into the desert to hunt ostriches, wild bulls, gazelles, and even lions. Waterbirds such as ducks were caught using boomerang-style weapons to knock them out of the sky – specially trained cats or dogs were sent to retrieve them. As he grew older, Tutankhamun was taught to throw a spear and fire arrows from a bow, so that he too could join the hunts. Sometimes the Egyptians would play ball games, but they were throwing games, not kicking ones, because the balls were made of heavy clay! On less active days, wealthy Egyptians were entertained by storytellers. They would sit down in the shade and listen to tales that had been passed down from generation to generation.

My favourite game by Tutankhamun *

Now that I'm getting older, I'm learning to hunt and to play grown-up board games like senet. My people love to play senet – I'm told that workers even play it by scratching a board into the sand and using stones as counters. My favourite board was specially made for me from dark ebony wood and the finest white elephant's ivory. To win the game you have to beat the forces of evil. I was taught how to play by my father and now I am getting so good that I can almost beat him!

* As Tutankhamun might have said...

Farming and transport

Unlike Tutankhamun and his fellow nobles, ordinary Egyptians had little spare time for games or hunting. Most people were farmers who spent their days hard at work in the fields, growing food for everyone else to eat. The most important crops were wheat and barley, which were used to make bread and beer, and **flax**, which was turned into ropes, mats, and **linen** cloth. Farmers also kept sheep, goats, geese, and other animals, as well as growing beans and lentils, and vegetables such as onions, lettuces, leeks, and garlic. Many different fruits were grown too, including melons, figs, dates, grapes, and pomegranates.

FLOODWATERS

Egyptian farmers built reservoirs to catch water when the Nile flooded. Using a device called a **shaduf**, they then transferred the floodwater from the reservoirs into canals they had dug. The water could then flow along the canals and into their parched fields.

Crops won't grow without water, however, and Egypt is a very hot country where it hardly ever rains. Farming was only possible because the river Nile usually flooded in summer, breaking its banks and covering the farmers' fields in water and rich, dark river mud. When the waters went down again, the ground was ideal for sowing crops. In bad years, when the river didn't rise high enough to flood, people went hungry. The ancient Egyptians believed their ruler could control the river, and one of the pharaoh's most important jobs was to perform special ceremonies every summer to encourage the Nile to rise and flood the fields.

The River Nile by Tutankhamun *

Our great river Nile is more important to me than all my glittering gold. Its life-giving water helps our food to grow, and this watery highway lets boats travel the entire length of Egypt swiftly and easily. When I go down to the river bank I see all sorts of boats passing by from small papyrus fishing canoes to huge wooden boats with big square sails. My family doesn't travel on the river much, because my father never leaves Akhetaten. But one day I'm going to have a big boat of my own and sail away to see the rest of my kingdom.

* When he was lazing by the river, we think Tutankhamun might have written this!

A FAVOURITE DRINK

Ordinary people didn't eat much in the way of fancy food, getting by mainly on bread, fish, and vegetables. But all Egyptians drank beer, even the children! The beer was flavoured with honey and spices, but was so lumpy it had to be sucked up through a wooden strainer which was a bit like a straw.

Pharaoh Tutankhamun

When Tutankhamun was only about nine years old, his childhood came to a sudden end. Akhenaten died, and Tutankhamun was now the ruler of the great land of Egypt. The prince sailed southwards from Akhetaten to the old capital city of Thebes, where he was crowned pharaoh by the priests in the great temple at **Karnak**. The ancient Egyptians believed that their pharaoh was more than just an ordinary man – he was thought to be a living god. He was head of the priesthood, the government, the law courts, and the army. Everyone and everything in Egypt belonged to him.

A PHARAOH'S EQUIPMENT

*A pharaoh didn't just wear a crown. On special occasions, he also carried a hooked **crook** and a whip-like **flail**. Sometimes he would also wear a false wooden beard and have the tail of a bull or a giraffe fixed to the back of his belt.*

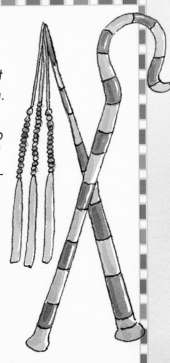

A pharaoh couldn't run the entire country single-handedly though, and there were lots of government officials to carry out the day-to-day business. Usually, these officials would consult with the pharaoh before taking important decisions, but Tutankhamun was too young and inexperienced to take control of the government and make his officials listen to him. He was pharaoh in name only. Throughout his reign, the real power lay in the hands of his chief minister, **Ay**, and the commander of his army, **Horemheb**.

It's tough being pharaoh! by Tutankhamun *

It's great to get out of Akhetaten, but Thebes is a little scary. It's a much bigger and noisier city, jam-packed with people hustling and bustling about their business. Being pharaoh is a little scary, too. I can't move without people watching me and, although I'm supposed to be giving the orders, nobody much listens. From the moment I wake up, everything I do is organized for me. I can't even just have a normal wash anymore – now that I'm a living god I have to start the day with a special purification ceremony. There are lots of other weird things about being a god. For example, people believe that it's bad luck if my shadow falls on them, and that it's an honour to kiss the ground before my feet!

* This is what we think Tutankhamun might have thought about being pharaoh...

CROWNS

*As pharaoh, Tutankhamun wore lots of different crowns. On special occasions, such as his coronation, he'd wear the red and white Double Crown (which combined the White Crown of **Upper Egypt** and the Red Crown of **Lower Egypt**) to show he was the lord of the two lands. For other state duties he wore the Blue Crown of the **New Kingdom** pharaohs, and for everyday use he would put on a stripey cloth headdress called a **nemes**.*

A marriage banquet

Soon after he became pharaoh, the nine-year-old Tutankhamun was married to his half-sister, **Ankhesenamun**. The new, young queen was actually higher in the royal line than her husband, as she was the daughter of Akhenaten and his chief wife Nefertiti. The ancient Egyptians didn't have any special wedding ceremonies – the young couple just moved in together and if they could afford it, they celebrated with a special meal. The marriage banquet of Tutankhamun and Ankhesenamun would have been a splendid royal affair.

Anyone who was anyone would have attended Tutankhamun's wedding feast, all wearing their finest clothes and jewellery. The men and women sat separately, and were served a sumptuous menu – exotic meats, such as gazelle and heron, fresh fruits, such as figs and watermelon, and all sorts of delicious cakes and pastries. To wash it down, there was a never-ending flow of beer and wine. Musicians played during the banquet to entertain the guests, and after everyone finished eating there were thrilling performances from singers and dancers, acrobats, and even magicians!

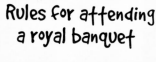

Rules for attending a royal banquet

Don't forget your manners. Only speak when you're spoken to, and never stare at other guests!

If eating with your fingers makes them sticky, call a servant to bring water for you to rinse them in.

Never get carried away and join in with the singers or dancers. Stay in your seat and keep your mouth shut!

Don't worry if you eat or drink too much. A servant will bring you a bowl to be sick in. Then you can go on partying!

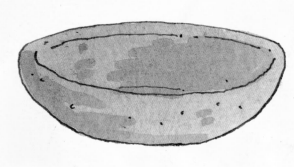

MUSICAL INSTRUMENTS

Egyptian musicians blew flutes and plucked harps or lutes (as shown). They also clicked castanet-like clappers, shook rattles, beat tambourines, or simply clapped their hands in time to the music.

clothes and cosmetics

As pharaoh, Tutankhamun had the best his country could offer from furniture and food to clothes, cosmetics, and jewellery. But even Tutankhamun didn't have to put on many clothes when he got up in the morning because Egypt is such a hot country. Like other noblemen, he wore a knee-length or ankle-length kilt, and his only underwear was a loincloth. Sometimes he'd add a T-shirt-shaped tunic, and on cool evenings he'd wrap himself up snugly in a cloak. Noblewomen wore long dresses with a shawl wrapped around their shoulders and tied under their breasts.

Tut's top grooming tips

1. Start the day by getting a slave to give you an all-over wash and massage.

2. Mix porridge and incense into a ball for a powerful underarm deodorant.

3. To clean your teeth, have a good long chew on a piece of tree root and gargle with a milk and herb mouthwash.

4. Use orange-tinted face paint to give your skin that fashionable dark colour (women should use a paler yellow tinted paint).

5. Outline your eyes with black or green paint. It will make them look bigger and protect them from disease. Make yourself a shiny red lip gloss from animal fat and red earth.

Wealthy Egyptians' clothes were made of the finest white linen – often so fine that it was see-through! Ordinary people had simpler clothes made of thicker, rougher cloth and very young children wore no clothes at all. Sandals were worn by the rich and poor and were woven from reeds, including papyrus. Make-up and the latest hairstyles were just as important as fine clothes – nobles would either wear a wig or spend hours having their own hair curled or plaited. In ancient Egypt, men and women wore make-up. The most important items in Tutankhamun's make-up box would have been the pots for his green and black eye-paints, and the tools for putting them on.

Restoring the old ways

Guided by his chief minister Ay, one of Tutankhamun's first acts as pharaoh was to put a stop to the worship of Akhenaten's single god, Aten. He restored all the old gods and all traces of Akhenaten and Aten were swept away. Aten's temples were pulled down, and Akhenaten's name was hacked from his statues and wall-carvings. Amun-Re became the chief god of ancient Egypt once again. All the old temples were repaired and the priests moved back in and began to worship the old gods. New temples were built, as well, to show Tutankhamun's respect for Amun-Re and the old gods.

LIFE AS A PRIEST

Ancient Egyptian priests often worked part-time – about one month in every four. When on duty in the temple, they were supposed to keep themselves pure for the god by washing often and shaving all the hair from their body – even their eyebrows!

The commander of Tutankhamun's army, Horemheb, was busy, too. Akhenaten had paid little attention to what was happening outside his city of Akhetaten, and by the time Tutankhamun came to the throne, Egypt's borders were under threat from some of its neighbours. Military outposts were under attack, and trading ships were being stopped from carrying goods in or out of Egyptian ports. Horemheb retrained the army and organized new weaponry and equipment, then sent his soldiers to sort out the problems. Meanwhile, the city of Akhetaten was abandoned and Thebes was reinstated as the capital city of Egypt.

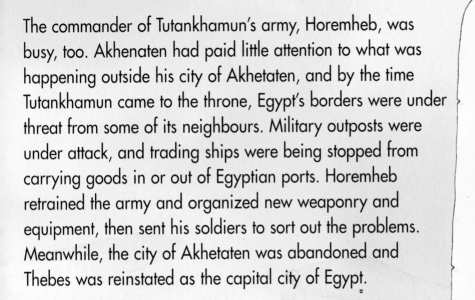

Tut's handy god guide

With over 1,000 gods, it's often tricky telling them apart. Here's a handy guide to some of the top gods:

Mut, Amun-Re's queen

Anubis, guardian of the dead

Hathor, goddess of love

Sobek, god of water and rivers

Taweret, protector of women and children

Thoth, god of scribes and learning

THE GOD OF HOMES AND FAMILIES

Ordinary people weren't allowed inside temples to worship. Instead they prayed at small local shrines or in their houses, often to statues of **Bes**, the protector of homes and families. Bes was half lion and half dwarf, and people believed he could scare away evil spirits.

Death of Tutankhamun

Sadly Tutankhamun didn't live long enough to make his own decisions as pharaoh. In 1327 BC, when he was about 17 or 18 years old, he suddenly died. The ancient Egyptians believed that the dead travelled to another world, called the **Afterlife**. In order to enjoy this special place, the dead would need their bodies. So the Egyptians developed a **mummification** process. Salts called **natron** were used to dry the dead bodies out and stop them from rotting away – preserving them forever. When the 40-day mummification process was complete, Tutankhamun's wife, Ankhesenamun, together with priests, government ministers, and his people gathered for the funeral on the west bank of the Nile, across the river from Thebes.

Modern day X-rays show that Tutankhamun was killed by a blow to the head. This might have been an accident, but some experts believe he was murdered – perhaps by his chief minister, Ay, who became pharaoh afterwards.

24

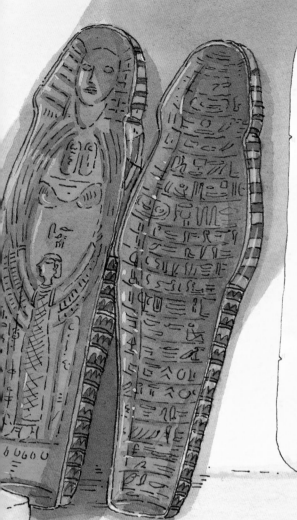

Instructions for making a mummy

1. Hook the brain out through the nose and throw it away.

2. Take out and keep the heart, lungs, stomach, liver, and intestines.

3. Cover the organs and body with plenty of natron salt.

4. Seal the lungs, liver, stomach, and intestines inside four special containers, called canopic jars.

5. The body will be ready after 40 days. Clean off the natron and tuck the heart back inside. Stuff the body with linen or sawdust and sweet-smelling herbs. Rub the skin with oils to soften it, then apply a waterproof coating of plant resins.

6. Last but not least, wrap the body up nice and tight in the finest linen bandages you can afford.

While women wailed and tore their clothes, the other mourners walked beside the funeral sledge carrying Tutankhamun's mummy to his tomb – a corridor and rooms cut into the rocky hillside of the **Valley of the Kings**. The tomb contained all the clothes, furniture, and other possessions he would need in the Afterlife. Here, priests carried out rituals, such as the **opening-of-the-mouth ceremony** which they believed allowed the dead to breathe, see, and hear again. Tutankhamun's body was placed inside a nest of three coffins which were then put inside a stone case called a **sarcophagus**. Finally, workmen built walls to seal the tomb doors and, they hoped, hide Tutankhamun's last resting place from robbers.

ANIMAL MUMMIES

The ancient Egyptians didn't just mummify their pharaohs. Anyone who could afford it was mummified. People even had their favourite pets mummified – birds, fish, and, of course, cats.

The lost tomb

Tutankhamun wasn't the only ancient Egyptian pharaoh to be laid to rest in the Valley of the Kings. Other rulers, their families, and government ministers were also buried there. Over time, the whereabouts of their tombs were forgotten, and it wasn't until the late 1890s that **Egyptologists** began to rediscover them. However, they were disappointed to find that robbers had broken into all of the tombs in ancient times, stealing or destroying the precious goods inside. By 1917, most people thought there was nothing more to be found in the Valley, but a British **archaeologist** was certain that one more tomb still lay hidden – that of the boy pharaoh Tutankhamun.

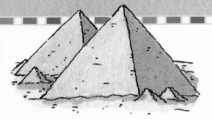

TOMB ROBBERS

Protecting the tombs of the dead pharaohs was a big problem in ancient Egypt. The early pharaohs built huge pyramids containing secret doors, tunnels, and traps to stop robbers from finding their precious possessions. When this didn't work, later pharaohs had secret tombs carved in the rocky cliffs of a place called the Valley of the Kings, but again most of the tombs were soon discovered and raided. Tomb robbing was a risky business though, because the punishment if caught was death. Robbers who were captured had to choose the way in which they died – being burnt alive or impaled on a stake.

The archaeologist's name was **Howard Carter,** and in 1917 he began his search for Tutankhamun's tomb. The excavation was funded by a wealthy British aristocrat called Lord Carnarvon, and during the next five years Carter's army of Egyptian workers shifted thousands of tons of sand and rubble – but found nothing. Then, on November 4, 1922, a stone step was uncovered. More digging revealed a stairway leading down to a sealed doorway. Howard sent an urgent telegraph message back to England telling Carnarvon to come to Egypt. Finally, towards the end of November, the pair watched as the doorway was opened – they had found Tutankhamun's long-lost tomb. But had robbers been inside before them?

My first glimpse of treasure by Howard carter *

It took a couple of days to clear the corridor into Tutankhamun's tomb. At its end, we discovered another sealed doorway. By late afternoon of November 26, we had scraped a small hole through the plaster and stone. We were full of hope, but had no clue about what to expect in the room beyond. I raised a candle to peer through the hole. At first I could see nothing, the hot air escaping from the chamber caused the candle flame to flicker, but presently, as my eyes grew accustomed to the light, details of the room emerged slowly from the mist, strange animals, statues, and gold – everywhere the glint of gold.

* Based on the journals of Howard carter

Tutankhamun's treasure

Howard Carter discovered that although robbers had broken into Tutankhamun's tomb just a few years after the funeral, most of the pharaoh's treasure was still there – including his throne and solid gold coffin! Everything that Tutankhamun would need in the Afterlife had been buried with him, egg-shaped boxes of food, furniture, and chests packed with his most precious possessions. Inside the antechamber alone, there were the wheels and bodies of four magnificent war chariots, and three ceremonial couches with their legs and sides carved in the shape of animals. It took Carter and his team nearly ten years to empty the tomb.

This is how Howard Carter's notes may have looked...

The Antechamber

The burial chamber
Inside we found four gilded shrines (huge box-like rooms), each one inside the other. Inside the fourth was Tutankhamun's carved stone sarcophagus, with its nest of three coffins.

The Shrines

The Sarcophagus

28

All of the wonderful treasures were carefully catalogued and then slowly transported down the Nile to the Cairo Museum. Buried with Tutankhamun were ceremonial objects that tell us about ancient Egyptian religious beliefs, and furniture that shows us how homes were decorated. We can learn about transport from his chariots and the 35 model boats buried with him. Also in his tomb were weapons, musical instruments, writing and tool kits, games such as senet, toys, and masses of beautiful jewellery and clothes – everything from sandals to a triangular linen loincloth! Much of what we now know about life in ancient Egyptian times has come from the goods found buried in tombs, and Pharaoh Tutankhamun's tomb was the greatest find of all time.

Plan of the tomb

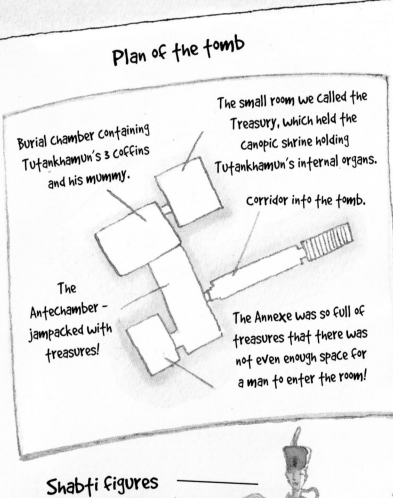

Burial chamber containing Tutankhamun's 3 coffins and his mummy.

The small room we called the Treasury, which held the canopic shrine holding Tutankhamun's internal organs.

Corridor into the tomb.

The Antechamber – jampacked with treasures!

The Annexe was so full of treasures that there was not even enough space for a man to enter the room!

The Death Mask

Tutankhamun's outer coffin was made of wood gilded with gold leaf. The second coffin was gilded wood too, but inlaid with pieces of pottery and glass. When we reached the third and final coffin we discovered it was made of solid gold. Inside was Tutankhamun's mummy, its face covered by a life-like golden mask.

Shabti figures

To provide the dead with servants for the Afterlife, small statues called shabtis were buried in tombs. Most people just had one or two shabti figures, but in Tutankhamun's tomb we found an astonishing 413!

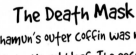

Glossary

AFTERLIFE The Egyptian idea of heaven. If you had led a good life you went there when you died – but only after passing a series of tests.

AKHENATEN Tutankhamun's father. He reigned as pharaoh 1352–1336 BC.

AKHETATEN Egyptian capital city built by Pharaoh Akhenaten.

AMARNA ART A new art style developed during the reign of Akhenaten.

AMUN-RE (RA) The chief god of ancient Egypt.

ANKHESENAMUN Tutankhamun's wife and half-sister.

ANUBIS The ancient Egyptian god believed to be the protector of the dead.

ARCHAEOLOGISTS People who dig up and study ancient ruins and remains.

ASTRONOMY The study of stars, planets, and the universe.

ATEN The sun god worshipped by Akhenaten. It was believed that he created and cared for mankind.

AY Tutankhamun's chief government minister.

BES The ancient Egyptian god of homes and the family.

CARTER (HOWARD) The archaeologist who discovered Tutankhamun's tomb.

CHARIOTEER A chariot driver.

CROOK A short stick with a curved top carried by the pharaoh. It was a symbol of the pharaoh's kingship.

EGYPTOLOGISTS People who study ancient Egypt.

FLAIL A string of beads on a stick carried by the pharaoh. It was a symbol of the fertility of the land.

FLAX A plant grown for its strong, woody fibre. The fibre was used to make ropes, mats, and linen cloth.

HATHOR The ancient Egyptian goddess of love.

HIEROGLYPHS The writing of ancient Egypt, made up of over 700 pictures and images.

HOREMHEB The commander of Tutankhamun's army.

KARNAK The biggest and most important Egyptian Temple, dedicated to the god Amun-Re.

KIYA One of Akhenaten's wives and Tutankhamun's mother.

LINEN A cloth woven from the fibres of the flax plant.

LOWER EGYPT The low-lying northern part of Egypt.

MUMMIFICATION The process used to preserve the bodies of the dead.

MUT An ancient Egyptian goddess, the wife of Amun-Re.

NATRON Salts collected from lakes in ancient Egypt. They were used to dry out dead bodies.

NEFERTITI Akhenaten's chief wife and mother of Ankhesenamun.

NEMES The pharaoh's everyday headdress. It was made from stripey cloth.

NEW KINGDOM The period in ancient Egyptian history between 1550–1069 BC.

NILE The main river that runs through Egypt.

OPENING-OF-THE-MOUTH CEREMONY A ceremony performed on a dead person to give their mummy the power of speech and movement in the Afterlife.

PAPYRUS A reed that grew on the banks of the river Nile.

PHARAOH An ancient

Egyptian king.

SARCOPHAGUS A large stone box in which the coffin was placed.

SCRIBES Men in ancient Egypt who could read and write.

SHADUF A device used by farmers to transfer flood water from reservoirs into canals, to water the fields.

SOBEK The ancient Egyptian god of water and rivers.

TAWERET The ancient Egyptian goddess of women and children.

TELL EL-AMARNA Modern day name for the ruins of the ancient Egyptian city of Akhetaten.

THEBES The capital city of ancient Egypt, now called Luxor.

THOTH The ancient Egyptian god of scribes and learning.

UPPER EGYPT The southern part of Egypt.

VALLEY OF THE KINGS A valley near Thebes. Many Egyptian kings were buried here in secret tombs carved out of the rock.

Index